CHIMPANZEES

LIVING WILD

Published by Creative Education
P.O. Box 227, Mankato, Minnesota 56002
Creative Education is an imprint of The Creative Company
www.thecreativecompany.us

Design and production by Mary Herrmann
Art direction by Rita Marshall
Printed in the United States of America

Photographs by Alamy (Arco Images GmbH, BRUCE COLEMAN INC., James Caldwell, Nick Greaves, Juniors Bildarchiv GmbH, Old Visuals, Steve Bloom Images), Dreamstime (Kitchner Bain, Lukas Blazek, Geraldine Doran, Ecoimagesphotos, Sefi Greiver, Iorboaz, Dmitry Kuznetsov, Natalia Stepanova, Anke Van Wyk, Robin Winkelman, Zepherwind), ellioti.org, Getty Images (Hulton Archive), iStockphoto (Steven Allan, Guenter Guni), Shutterstock (Alessandrozocc, Kitch Bain, Sara Berdon, Nick Biemans, Bierchen, Norma Cornes, costas anton dumitrescu, JKlingebiel, JONG KIAM SOON, PRILL Mediendesign und Fotografie, Uryadnikov Sergey, Ronald van der Beek, Dana Ward, Y. F. Wong), Wikipedia (Didier Descouens, Ikiwaner, NASA)

Library of Congress Cataloging-in-Publication Data
Gish, Melissa.
Chimpanzees / by Melissa Gish.
p. cm. — (Living wild)
Includes index.
Summary: A look at chimpanzees, including their habitats, physical characteristics such as their knuckle-walking, behaviors, relationships with humans, and protected status in the world today.
ISBN 978-1-60818-286-2
1. Chimpanzees—Juvenile literature. I. Title.

QL737.P96G5535 2013
599.885—dc23   2012023306

First Edition
9 8 7 6 5 4 3 2 1

CREATIVE EDUCATION

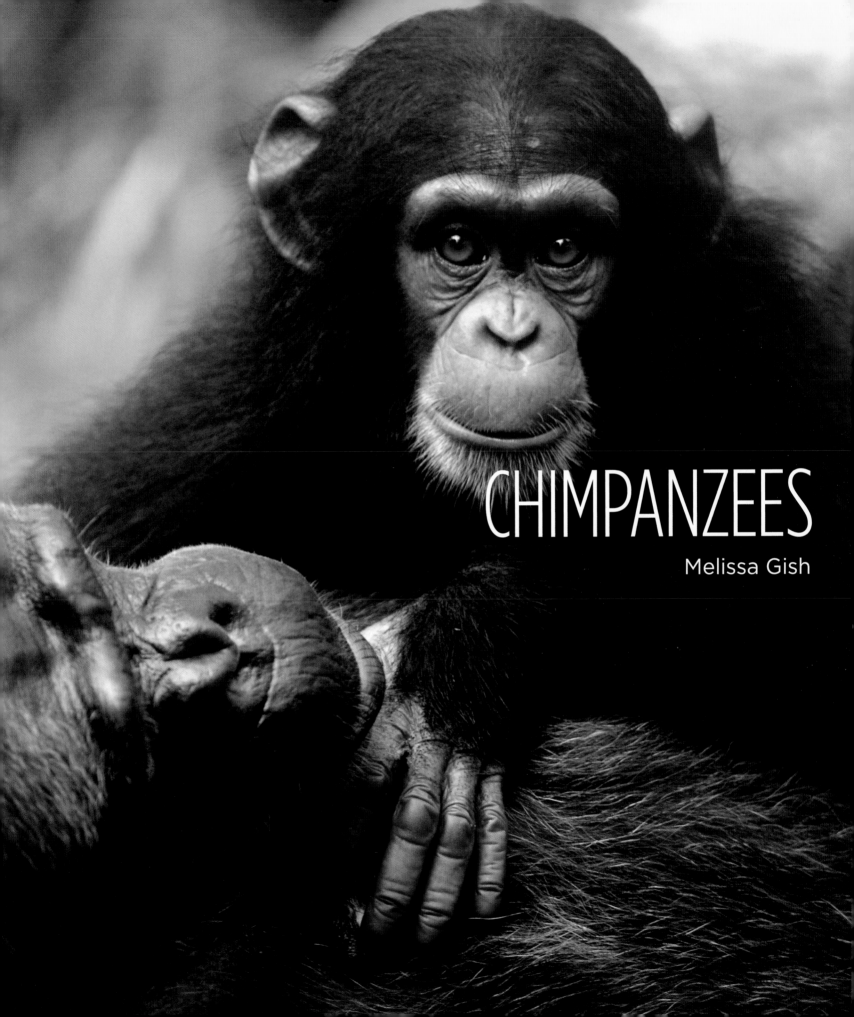

CHIMPANZEES

Melissa Gish

In Uganda's Kibale National Park, under the canopy of fruit trees, a group of chimpanzees groom

each other, cleaning dry skin and seeds from their fur.

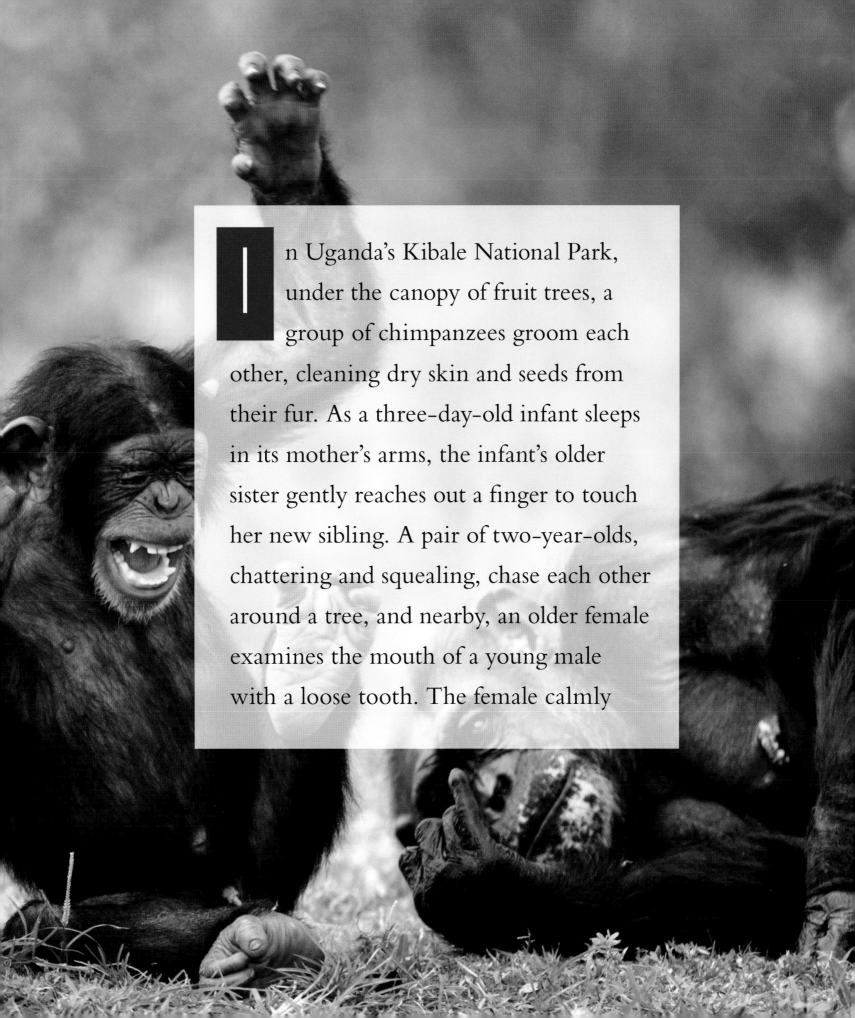

In Uganda's Kibale National Park, under the canopy of fruit trees, a group of chimpanzees groom each other, cleaning dry skin and seeds from their fur. As a three-day-old infant sleeps in its mother's arms, the infant's older sister gently reaches out a finger to touch her new sibling. A pair of two-year-olds, chattering and squealing, chase each other around a tree, and nearby, an older female examines the mouth of a young male with a loose tooth. The female calmly picks up a twig and begins cleaning around the tooth. Suddenly, a leopard bursts from the underbrush. Screaming and hooting, the females and young take to the trees. The adult males rush toward the leopard, shrieking, waving sticks, and throwing rocks at the intruder. Despite its hunger, the leopard quickly realizes it is no match for the mob of chimpanzees. It dashes away into the forest to wait until dark, when it will try again.

WHERE IN THE WORLD THEY LIVE

Central Chimpanzee
Gabon, Democratic Republic of the Congo

Western Chimpanzee
Guinea to western Nigeria

Eastern Chimpanzee
Uganda and Kenya to Zambia

Nigeria-Cameroon Chimpanzee
Nigeria, Cameroon

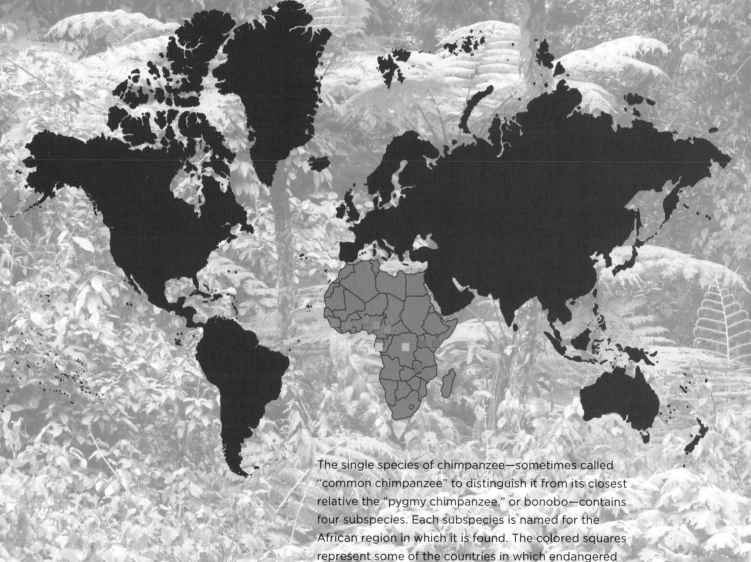

The single species of chimpanzee—sometimes called "common chimpanzee" to distinguish it from its closest relative the "pygmy chimpanzee," or bonobo—contains four subspecies. Each subspecies is named for the African region in which it is found. The colored squares represent some of the countries in which endangered chimpanzees live today.

JUNGLE GYMNASTS

Chimpanzees are found in woodlands and rainforests on the continent of Africa. In 1488, Portuguese explorer Duarte Pacheco Pererira visited what is now Cameroon and Equatorial Guinea on the west coast of Africa and may have been the first European to see chimpanzees. He recorded his experiences in a 1506 diary of his journeys, but it was not until the early 18th century, when Portuguese colonists settled in what is now Angola, that the name "chimpanzee" was documented. It originated from the Luba-Kasai word *kivili-chimpenze*, which translates to "mock man." Luba-Kasai is a language spoken in Angola and the neighboring Democratic Republic of the Congo.

The common chimpanzee (*Pan troglodytes*) belongs to the group of **mammals** called primates, animals with large brains and gripping hands. Lemurs, lorises, tarsiers, monkeys, apes, and humans are all primates. The chimpanzee's closest relative is another ape, the bonobo (*Pan paniscus*). In general, bonobos are slightly slimmer than common chimpanzees, which led to their nickname, "pygmy chimpanzee," and they

Orangutans are more solitary than other apes, and only the mother and offspring share a strong bond.

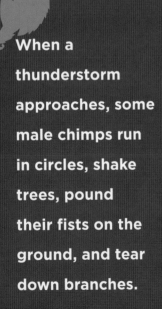

When a thunderstorm approaches, some male chimps run in circles, shake trees, pound their fists on the ground, and tear down branches.

have slightly smaller heads and ears. Bonobos—once more widespread—are now found only in the humid rainforests of the Democratic Republic of the Congo.

Chimpanzees were once abundant throughout Africa; however, today they can be found in only about half the number of places they once inhabited. There are four subspecies of common chimpanzee, which are named for the animals' geographic locations: the western chimpanzee, found from Guinea to western Nigeria; the Nigeria-Cameroon chimpanzee, found in those nations; the central chimpanzee, found from Gabon to the Democratic Republic of the Congo; and the eastern chimpanzee, found from Uganda and Kenya south to Zambia.

As apes, chimpanzees are related to gorillas and orangutans, but they are even more closely related to humans. Recently, an international group of 67 researchers, working together in the Chimpanzee Sequencing and Analysis Consortium, established through **DNA** research that chimpanzees share 96 percent of human DNA—which is more than they share with other apes.

Apes are sometimes confused with monkeys, but the two animals are very different from one another. Apes

Chimpanzees communicate by hooting, a sound that can be heard from up to two miles (3.2 km) away.

Like larger apes such as gorillas, chimps knuckle-walk, which allows them to carry objects in their hands while mobile.

are tailless and have flat noses, while monkeys have tails and snouts. Additionally, apes have much larger brains and are more intelligent than monkeys. Chimpanzees are considered the most intelligent of all apes. They are also capable of standing upright, but they walk on their hind feet and the knuckles of their hands most of the time. This is called knuckle-walking, and gorillas and chimpanzees are the only primates to move this way.

Chimpanzees are covered with black hair except on their faces, ears, and the palms of their hands and feet. Males average just over 5 feet (1.5 m) tall and weigh up to 140 pounds (63.5 kg). Females are generally smaller than males. They average just over 4 feet (1.2 m) tall and weigh 70 to 100 pounds (31.8–45.4 kg). A chimpanzee's arms are longer than its legs, and like humans and other apes, chimpanzees have four fingers and a thumb on each hand and five toes on each foot. Their fingers and thumbs give chimpanzees a strong grip and the ability to hold and manipulate objects with **dexterity**. Instead of claws, they have fingernails and toenails, which they bite to keep trimmed. All these features allow chimpanzees to swing through trees as they browse for food.

Great apes (chimps, bonobos, gorillas, orangutans, and humans) have an opposable hallux, or big toe.

Overhunting by chimpanzees is causing a steady and serious decline in the red colobus monkey population.

The Honolulu Zoo provides its chimps with artificial termite mounds filled with primate food that keep the animals busy for hours.

Contrary to the popular belief that chimpanzees *live* in trees, chimpanzees actually spend most of their time traveling on foot and may trek up to six miles (9.7 km) each day in search of food. They typically rise before dawn to begin searching for food. They can remember where the best fruit grows, and their ability to differentiate between colors allows them to monitor when fruit becomes ripe.

Chimpanzees have a high **metabolism** and are able to easily digest a wide variety of food. They are omnivores, meaning they eat both vegetation and meat. Roughly half their diet is composed of fruit. They also eat seeds, bark, insects, bird eggs and hatchlings, shellfish, and small mammals—depending on the region and season. Chimpanzees in western and central Africa have been observed hunting cooperatively to bring down colobus monkeys, their main source of meat in that region.

They get much of the moisture they need from their food, but chimpanzees also ingest water, typically using mashed up leaves like a sponge to sop up water from a pool. A favorite food is termites, which can be difficult to obtain since these insects burrow deep in the hard, muddy nests they

Chimps today are using improved termite fishing tools with brush-like tips, which catch more termites.

Sometimes chimps combine their "fishing" technique with drilling, forcing a larger stick into the termite mound to open a hole.

construct in the ground. To reach termites, a chimpanzee locates a long, stiff stem, strips it of its leaves, and inserts it into a hole in a termite nest. The insects, instinctively acting to protect the nest, bite the stem. The chimpanzee then withdraws the stem, now covered with termites, and eats the insects. This behavior was the first example of chimpanzee toolmaking ever observed by humans.

Chimpanzees spend their days foraging, grooming, napping, and playing. They sleep about eight hours a night. As the sun goes down, a chimpanzee will select a spot high in a tree and build a springy, bowl-shaped nest of leaves and branches. Chimpanzees build a new nest each night and call to each other to let everyone in their group know their whereabouts. Chimpanzees are vulnerable while sleeping. One of their deadliest predators is the python, a snake that grows to 20 feet (6.1 m) in length and kills by wrapping itself around prey and suffocating it. A python can swallow a young chimpanzee whole.

Many chimpanzee habitats are shared by ground-dwelling baboons. Baboons and chimpanzees accept each other as equals and sometimes share food. The young of both species often play together, which is rare among animals of different species. A common predator of both chimpanzees and baboons is the leopard, a stealthy cat that ambushes its prey. Baboons have better eyesight than chimpanzees and will warn chimpanzees of predators hidden in underbrush. Likewise, baboons rely on chimpanzees to scout the land from trees and warn them of danger. Studies have shown that baboons and chimpanzees appear to understand one another's calls, leading these animals to form alliances that serve both their communities.

A 2008 study in Tanzania revealed that chimps have an instinctive fear of predatory snakes in the wild.

Chimps are the only animals that make tools by taking an object and turning it into something that can be used for a specific purpose.

THE APES

When the tribe saw that Kerchak's rage had ceased they came slowly down from their arboreal retreats and pursued again the various occupations which he had interrupted.

The young played and frolicked about among the trees and bushes. Some of the adults lay prone upon the soft mat of dead and decaying vegetation which covered the ground, while others turned over pieces of fallen branches and clods of earth in search of the small bugs and reptiles which formed a part of their food. . . .

They had passed an hour or so thus when Kerchak called them together, and, with a word of command to them to follow him, set off toward the sea.

They traveled for the most part upon the ground, where it was open, following the path of the great elephants whose comings and goings break the only roads through those tangled mazes of bush, vine, creeper, and tree. When they walked it was with a rolling, awkward motion, placing the knuckles of their closed hands upon the ground and swinging their ungainly bodies forward.

But when the way was through the lower trees they moved more swiftly, swinging from branch to branch with the agility of their smaller cousins, the monkeys. And all the way Kala carried her little dead baby hugged closely to her breast.

It was shortly after noon when they reached a ridge overlooking the beach where below them lay the tiny cottage which was Kerchak's goal.

He had seen many of his kind go to their deaths before the loud noise made by the little black stick in the hands of the strange white ape who lived in that wonderful lair, and Kerchak had made up his brute mind to own that death-dealing contrivance, and to explore the interior of the mysterious den.

excerpt from Tarzan of the Apes, *by Edgar R. Burroughs (1875–1950)*

CLIMBING THE FAMILY TREE

C himpanzees are highly social animals that form strong, lifelong bonds with one another. Their social structure is complex. Chimpanzees gather in groups, called communities, comprising as few as 15 or as many as 150 members. A chimpanzee community is led by a dominant male, called the alpha male, whose responsibilities include defending the community from other males that might want to take over, protecting young and weak members from predators, and maintaining peace within the community. The alpha regularly patrols his community's territory, which is typically a range of 11 to 13 square miles (28.5–33.7 sq km), and may call together the other males of his community to defend their territory against invading chimpanzees.

Community members spend time communicating, eating and playing together, and grooming one another. Grooming is the most important gesture in forming chimpanzee social bonds. It eases stress among community members, confirms old relationships, and establishes new ones. Communication is important as well. Similar to the way humans communicate, chimpanzees use facial

Chimpanzees spend about seven hours a day eating and teaching their young how to find the best food.

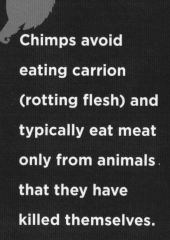

Chimps avoid eating carrion (rotting flesh) and typically eat meat only from animals that they have killed themselves.

A chimp that wants to become an alpha male must first gain acceptance from the females in a community.

Chimps recognize that aggressive males are less successful community leaders because calm males maintain peace among members.

expressions and body gestures in addition to vocalizations to show meaning, make requests, and give commands.

Primatologist Jane Goodall has identified 30 distinct chimpanzee sounds associated with clear meanings. While most animals direct vocalizations to the entire group, as a signal or warning, for example, chimpanzees vocalize individually in a manner similar to human conversation. This behavior has led some scientists to speculate that the chimpanzee's form of vocal communication may indicate the beginning of language.

For many days at a time, a chimpanzee community may break into smaller groups, called parties, to forage for food. In areas where food is abundant, parties may exceed 25 members, but where food is scarce, parties are composed of 3 to 10 members that spread out over an entire territory. Males may form gangs that move around together, kicking tree trunks as they travel to let other members of their community—and rival chimpanzees—know they are there.

Male chimpanzees are much more aggressive than females, who are highly affectionate with one another and with their offspring. Within a community, males challenge each other and may attempt to overthrow

the alpha male through such displays of aggression as throwing rocks, shaking branches, and charging at the alpha male. One of the opponents almost always backs down, so males rarely need to attack each other.

However, males often violently attack members of rival communities in order to gain control of territory. A 10-year study in Uganda's Kibale National Park revealed that male chimpanzee gangs routinely invade neighboring chimpanzee territories, beating rival males to death, eating infants, and integrating females into their

Research shows that male chimps wage war on rival communities an average of every 10 to 14 days.

Older chimps teach younger chimps which food is safe to eat and where the ripest fruit can be found.

own communities. Such a practice enables a conquering chimpanzee community to access more food to support more females, thus producing more offspring. The community could then grow larger and stronger—able to defend itself against future invasions.

Male gangs also hunt together. Although meat makes up less than 5 percent of a chimpanzee's typical diet, chimpanzees are still skillful cooperative hunters. They encircle an animal, closing in and giving it no way to escape. Then they leap on it, grab it by its hind legs, and smash its head against a hard surface to kill it. Most prey taken in this way—antelopes, wild boars, and monkeys—are juveniles. In 2007, University of Cambridge researchers in Senegal also observed chimpanzees fashioning spears from branches sharpened with their teeth and using these weapons to skewer monkeys in trees. This is another example of tool use, which is rare in most species besides humans. Chimpanzees eat meat mostly in the driest months—August and September—when fruit becomes scarce.

When food is abundant, rival chimpanzee communities sometimes mingle without conflict. Individuals may share food and play together, though adult males usually keep their distance from one another. Young females who have not yet given birth may even leave their community to join a rival community in search of mates. Scientists believe this behavior is an instinctive means of maintaining **genetic** diversity among chimpanzees.

Chimpanzees are able to mate at any time of year. When a community is gathered, the dominant male typically has his choice of females, but when a community is scattered or the alpha male is out on patrol, other males take advantage of his absence and pursue females. Chimpanzees may live up to 45 years in the wild (or up to 60 years in captivity). Males reach maturity around age 16. Females begin mating

Chimps pass on their knowledge of medicinal plants to treat upset stomachs, infections, and parasites from one generation to the next.

Mother chimpanzees may carry their babies everywhere they go for up to three years of the infant's life.

at around age 13, typically giving birth once every 5 to 6 years. Chimpanzees will not mate with siblings.

Baby chimpanzees develop inside their mothers for eight months before being born. This is just four weeks shorter than normal human **gestation**. A newborn chimpanzee is completely helpless. At first, the mother must hold the infant to her chest so it can feed on the milk she produces, but within just a few days it grows strong enough to grip the hair of its mother's chest by itself. At three months of age, it gets its first teeth, and at five to seven months old, it will ride on its mother's back as she moves through the forest. It can also walk on its hind legs while holding onto its mother.

A chimpanzee is unsteady on its feet for the first two years of its life. It will never stray far from its mother and will continue to nurse from her until it is four or five years old, when its permanent teeth start growing in. Only the female chimpanzees participate in the nurturing of baby chimpanzees. Immature females learn how to carry and groom babies by watching the more experienced females. Mothers and female siblings play with babies, swinging them by their arms and legs and

gently wrestling with them to help them build up their muscles. Although adult male chimpanzees do not seek out the attention of younger community members, they patiently allow babies to climb over them, pull their ears and limbs, and jump on them. Such playful activities help young chimpanzees become strong and confident members of their community.

Play helps chimps develop the social skills necessary to confront aggressive behaviors and other everyday problems.

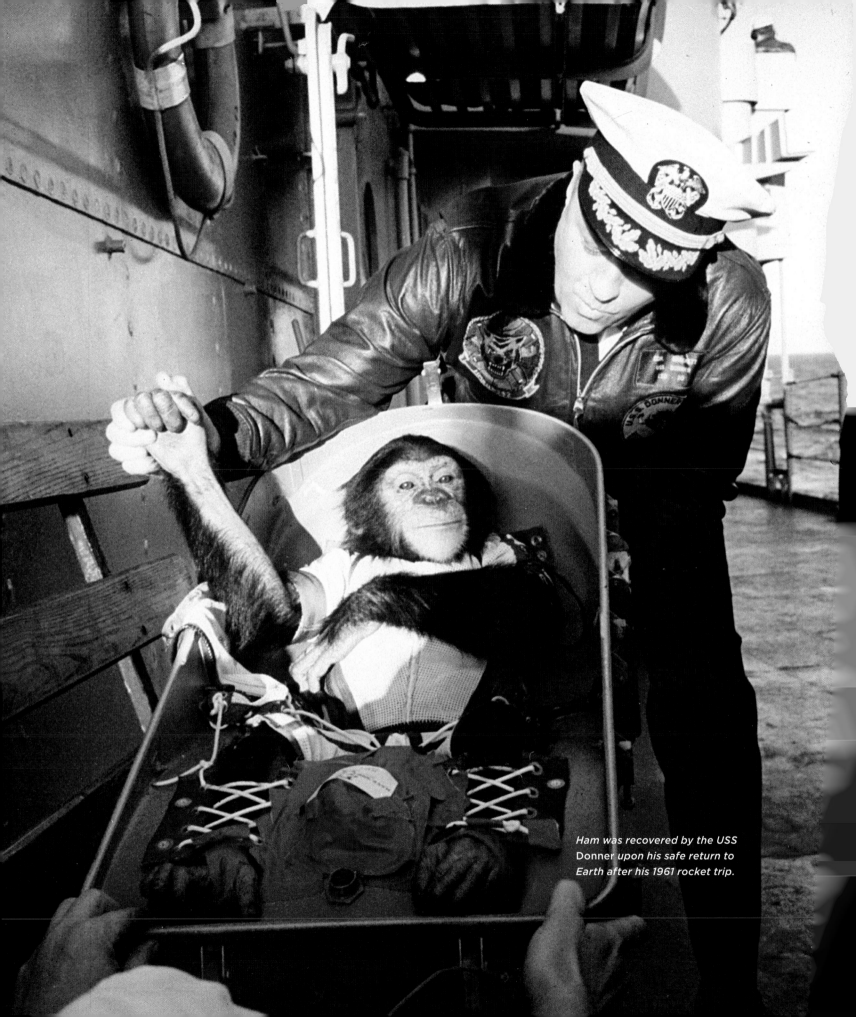

Ham was recovered by the USS Donner upon his safe return to Earth after his 1961 rocket trip.

GOING APE

C himpanzees—probably more than any other large mammal—are valued for their usefulness in science. Because chimpanzees are highly intelligent and their brains and skeletal structures are similar to those of humans, chimpanzees have been used in scientific research regarding topics from **cognitive** function to disease resistance to crash helmets. In the early years of chimpanzee research, many test subjects died under inhumane conditions, but today various laws protect chimpanzees from unnecessary suffering and death. In December 2011, the United States' National Institutes of Health (NIH) announced that it would approve of using chimpanzees for public health research only if no other methods were possible and only if the animals were housed in habitats that closely resembled a natural chimpanzee environment. Despite the NIH's guidelines, many animal rights groups object to the use of chimpanzees for any sort of scientific research because they believe that non-human primates should have human-like rights and be protected from torture.

The U.S. relied heavily on chimpanzees in early experiments on space travel. In 1959, Ham, a three-year-

Snooky the Chimp starred in several short, silent movies made in Hollywood during the early 1920s.

Female chimps may inherit high status in a community by showing loyalty to older females that are close to death.

A 2011 study at the Yerkes National Primate Research Center in Atlanta found that chimps choose to share food more often than not.

old chimpanzee captured in Cameroon, began National Aeronautics and Space Administration (NASA) training at Holloman Air Force Base in New Mexico. Most chimpanzee training required chimpanzees to perform repeated tasks, with the chimpanzees being punished for incorrect responses (by receiving an electric shock) and rewarded for correct actions (with banana-flavored treats). Ham became the first chimpanzee in space two years later. By executing simple tasks, such as pushing a lever, inside his tiny capsule, Ham proved at the time that chimpanzees—and most likely humans—could operate controls under the stress of space travel and return to Earth safely. Ten months later, five-year-old Enos became the first chimpanzee to **orbit** Earth, making two orbits before his capsule splashed down safely in the ocean. Enos's success paved the way for John Glenn's historic flight as the first American to orbit our planet.

Military experiments on chimpanzees were the focus of the 1987 movie *Project X*, which starred Matthew Broderick and more than a dozen real chimpanzee actors. The movie suggested that animal research was unnecessarily dangerous. The use of chimpanzees in the entertainment industry has come under fire recently as well. Because chimpanzees are smart and easy to train, they were once used extensively in movies and television—typically to play comedic roles. But according to animal trainers, animal actors may soon be a thing of the past. Computer-generated images of animals are now being used instead.

One of Hollywood's most chimp-heavy franchises has a history of using the fewest real chimpanzees in its productions. In 1963, French novelist Pierre Boulle introduced the world to *The Planet of the Apes*, a science fiction story that takes place hundreds of years in the future when an astronaut discovers walking, talking apes— chimpanzees, orangutans, and gorillas—ruling a distant planet, while humans are kept as slaves and pets. The book spawned five films from 1968 to 1973 and two television series that aired in the 1970s, but with the exception of the chimpanzee infants, all chimpanzee characters were played by humans in makeup. More recently, director Tim Burton reimagined the original story in his own version of *The Planet of the Apes* in 2001, and a scientific explanation for super intelligence in apes was suggested in the 2011 film *Rise of the Planet of the Apes*. Real chimpanzees were the

Lake Tanganyika is the world's longest lake and is the second deepest and second largest by volume.

Tanzania's Mahale Mountains National Park, home of the world's largest chimp population, can be reached only by boat from Lake Tanganyika.

The bush baby is called nagapie, or "little night monkey," in Afrikaans, a language spoken in South Africa.

Scientists believe that the earliest common ancestor of humans and chimps may have looked similar to a modern bush baby.

stars of DisneyNature's 2012 documentary *Chimpanzee*, which records the true story of an orphan named Oscar being adopted by an alpha male.

In the early days of Hollywood, however, chimpanzees were used often, particularly in action-adventure films featuring tropical locales. In 1914, the book *Tarzan of the Apes*, by American author Edgar Rice Burroughs, was published. The title character of Tarzan is orphaned in Africa and raised by a troop of great apes. Tarzan's story has become well known the world over. Numerous films, books, comics, and television shows have been produced over the years, showcasing Tarzan's complicated relationships with his ape family and human society. Although it never appeared in any of Burroughs's books, a chimpanzee character named Cheeta was introduced in the 1932 film *Tarzan the Ape Man*. This character was played by numerous real chimpanzee actors over the span of several decades, and Cheeta became Tarzan's best-known sidekick throughout the ape man's history.

Today, many chimpanzee actors have retired, and many more are expected to retire soon. Refuges such as C.H.E.E.T.A. (Creative Habitats and Enrichment for

Cheeta made his second film with Johnny Weissmuller (as Tarzan) in 1934's Tarzan and His Mate.

Endangered and Threatened Apes) Primate Sanctuary in California, the Center for Great Apes in Florida, and Save the Chimps sanctuaries located in New Mexico and Florida have been flooded with new residents in recent years. C.H.E.E.T.A., founded in 1991 by Hollywood animal trainer Dan Westfall, was named in honor of Tarzan's Cheeta, but it was established primarily for the real-life Cheeta, a former chimpanzee actor. Tony Gentry, Cheeta's owner and Westfall's uncle, was unhappy with the fact that many movie primates were sent to research facilities when the animals were no longer useful, so Westfall created C.H.E.E.T.A. Visitors to the

Chimps are encouraged to create art using pens, paints, and brushes at Chimp Haven near Shreveport, Louisiana.

website www.cheetathechimp.org can see pictures of the sanctuary's primates and examples of the paintings created by the resident chimpanzees—including Cheeta, who is thought to be more than 70 years old.

According to **zoologists** at sanctuaries and zoos, painting seems to be an activity that many captive chimpanzees enjoy. June, a chimpanzee at the Lincoln Park

Zoo in Chicago, started with finger painting but moved on to using a brush to paint works that have sold for as much as $1,400. The fictional chimpanzee Curious George, created in 1941 by German writer Margret Rey and her illustrator husband Hans Augusto Rey, also has a passion for finger painting—as well as for balloons, cheese, kites, bunnies, bouncy balls, and just about anything new he encounters in his many adventures. For decades, Curious George, who is identified as a chimpanzee despite his being called a monkey, has been the star of numerous television specials, movies, games, books, and toys.

Daring astronaut primates are featured on the television show *Captain Simian and the Space Monkeys*. In this animated adventure, one of NASA's space chimpanzees, Charlie, accidentally escapes orbit and flies across space and time. He reaches a planet where he is named Captain Charlie Simian and given super intelligence and high-tech weapons in exchange for his promise to rid the universe of an evil enemy. This scenario is not far from reality, as chimpanzees in the wild face equally dangerous enemies—humans— who threaten chimpanzee populations with habitat loss, **poaching**, and illegal capture.

In 2006, an art expert was fooled into thinking a painting by Banghi, a chimpanzee at Zoo Halle in Germany, was made by a human artist.

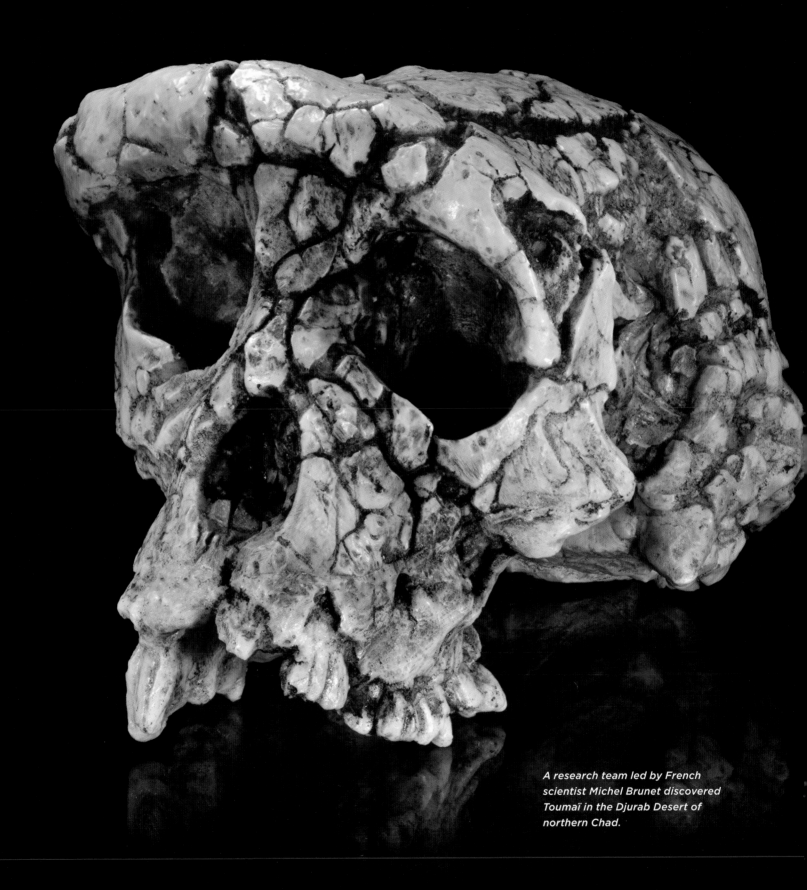

A research team led by French scientist Michel Brunet discovered Toumaï in the Djurab Desert of northern Chad.

CHALLENGING CHIMPANZEES

The deserts of northern Chad have yielded many important fossils but are much farther west of where scientists used to look.

H umans did not **evolve** from apes, but many scientists believe that chimpanzees, gorillas, and humans all came from a common ancestor that existed in Africa and southern Asia about 15 million years ago. Gorilla ancestors **diverged** from the line of shared chimpanzee and human ancestry about 12 million years ago, and then chimpanzees and humans split into 2 separate lines about 6 million years ago. In 2001 and 2002, anthropologists (scientists who study the history of humankind) discovered a skull, partial jaw, and some teeth of *Sahelanthropus*, nicknamed Toumaï (*tu-MY*), which means "hope of life" in Dazaga, the language of Chad, where the 7-million-year-old fossils were found. Some scientists believe this species is one of the last common ancestors of chimpanzees and humans before the two split into separate species.

Fossil evidence of chimpanzees has been sparse, mostly because the tropical forest environment of early chimpanzees was too acidic and rainy to preserve fossils. In 2005, American anthropologist Sally McBrearty found the first chimpanzee fossils, three 500,000-year-

Chimpanzees in zoos commonly learn new behaviors from humans and then teach them to their offspring.

old teeth, in Kenya. Also found nearby were fossils of human ancestors and stone tools, suggesting that early humans and chimpanzees shared the same environment—something that scientists previously thought unlikely. Discovering that humans and chimpanzees were part of the same ecosystem has encouraged further study of the Sahara Desert in Chad, which was once a forested wetland, and of the potential relationship between human ancestors and chimpanzees in the region.

According to researchers, chimpanzees were once abundant across their African ranges. About 100 years ago, nearly 2 million chimpanzees could be found in 25

African countries. Today, it is estimated that 172,000 to 300,000 chimpanzees exist in the wild. Outside Africa, chimpanzees have been found to be useful by scientists and featured on television and in the movies, but many people on the chimpanzees' home continent do not consider them anything special. This attitude is plainly reflected in the growth of the bushmeat trade, a business in which wild animals are hunted and sold as food.

Many animals currently hunted for bushmeat, such as chimpanzees, are protected by national and international laws, and the bushmeat trade is illegal in many regions of the world. However, the demand for food in **impoverished** countries has risen so dramatically that chimpanzees are now at risk. In addition to hunting, such human activities as logging, agriculture, and the expansion of cities are having devastating effects on primate populations. **Deforestation** of chimpanzee habitat to make farmland disrupts many primate groups, leading to their demise.

The illegal pet trade is another major threat to chimpanzees. While it is against the law in most parts of the world to own primate pets, many people still buy them. Poachers make so much money in this trade that they are

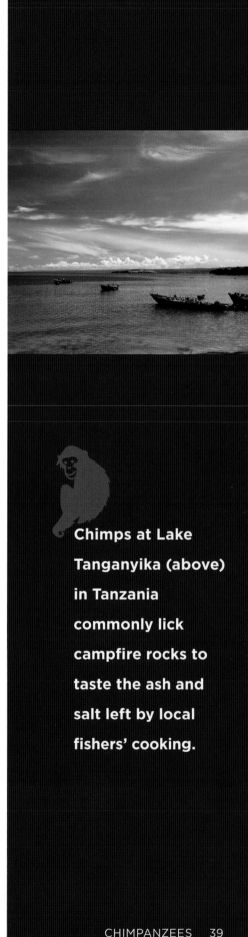

Chimps at Lake Tanganyika (above) in Tanzania commonly lick campfire rocks to taste the ash and salt left by local fishers' cooking.

Poachers kill adult chimpanzees for their meat, often leaving infants and juveniles orphaned and vulnerable.

willing to risk getting caught. But most poachers don't get caught. There simply aren't enough park rangers to patrol all the tropical forestland. And as long as people continue to buy illegal animals, poachers will continue to capture primates, often killing adults to steal their babies.

When captive chimpanzees become too old and strong to be kept as pets or used in the entertainment industry, they are often sold to research facilities around the world—many of which do not enforce the same anti-cruelty laws that exist in the U.S.—and never returned to the wild. Most pet chimpanzees are abandoned when they are around three years old and typically spend the rest of their lives in non-natural habitats where they never reproduce. Researchers predict that if the hunting, capturing, and **displacing** of apes and monkeys does not stop, 25 percent of the world's primate species—including chimpanzees—will be **extinct** by 2020.

Understanding chimpanzees is vital to saving the species. While much research focuses on the ways in which chimpanzees and humans are similar, such as how we communicate and form relationships with others of our kind, other chimpanzee studies strive to pinpoint major differences between our species. Such research has revealed that humans and chimpanzees utilize different problem-solving techniques and that, while humans can understand **abstract** concepts such as light and heavy, chimpanzees cannot comprehend these ideas. Physically, as humans age, our brains actually shrink, becoming less functional, but chimpanzees maintain full brain size and function throughout their lifetime. Such research may someday help scientists find ways to extend brain function in humans.

Perhaps the most significant contributions to global chimpanzee research began in 1960, when a young researcher named Jane Goodall went to Africa to study chimpanzees. Early in her investigation of chimpanzees at what was then the Gombe Stream Chimpanzee Reserve in western Tanzania, Goodall became the first to report tool use in chimpanzees, completely changing the way humans thought about the relationship between humans and chimpanzees. Until that time, only humans were believed to be capable of fashioning and using tools. Goodall also discovered that the chimpanzees she observed expressed emotions and had unique personalities.

Instead of identifying her research subjects by number,

Chimpanzee research may hold keys to understanding the evolution of early human behaviors and social structure.

Unlike most animals, chimps recognize their reflections in a mirror as their own bodies, a cognitive behavior that signals intelligence.

One-quarter of Tanzania's land is designated as protected areas, including Gombe Stream National Park.

as most scientists do, Goodall gave the chimpanzees names. Goliath was the first of a long line of alpha males of the community Goodall observed, and Fifi was a young female whom Goodall watched grow up and become a mother of nine offspring. Goodall discovered that chimpanzees form friendships, teaching each other how to use medicinal plants and operate tools to open nuts and capture prey. She found that chimpanzees are capable of random acts of kindness as well as shocking acts of brutality—much like humans.

What began as a six-month planned study in Gombe has become a lifelong mission for Goodall, who is now known the world over for her remarkable insights on chimpanzee intelligence, communication, and what many scientists consider the early stages of culture. In 1977, she founded the Jane Goodall Institute, a worldwide network of organizations whose combined mission is to save great apes by promoting education, preservation, and responsibility. Today, Goodall continues to travel around the world to speak about the environmental crisis and the urgent need for individuals to take action to preserve and protect our planet's natural resources—including chimpanzees and other great apes—before it is too late.

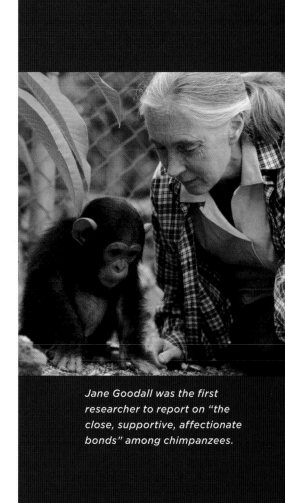

Jane Goodall was the first researcher to report on "the close, supportive, affectionate bonds" among chimpanzees.

ANIMAL TALE: THE GLUTTONOUS CHIMPANZEE

The nomadic Fulani people have traditionally made the sprawling savannas of western Africa their home, and their herds of cattle have shared the grasslands and watering holes with many wild animals—including savanna-dwelling chimpanzees. This Fulani folktale explains why the chimpanzee has no tail.

Long ago, Doondari, the creator of all things, made a splendid gift of long tails to Vervet, Mangabey, and the other monkeys—as well as to Chimpanzee. Chimpanzee and his cousins were pleased with their tails, which they used like a fifth limb when climbing. Doondari enjoyed watching his creatures playfully leap from tree to tree and dangle upside down from high branches.

The monkeys occasionally nibbled small fruit and munched tender leaves as they played, but Chimpanzee constantly leapt from tree to tree, stripping the branches of their fruit and nuts.

"What a glutton you are," called Doondari to Chimpanzee. "Save some food for your cousins," he commanded.

"I'm very sorry," said Chimpanzee, and, nodding in obedience, he slowed his eating—for a day.

The next morning he swung through the trees, using his tail to climb higher toward the best fruit. The monkeys watched their cousin grow fatter.

Soon Chimpanzee's body was bulky, and his limbs were thick. Yet he continued eating everything within reach.

"We're hungry, Chimpanzee," cried Vervet. "You have eaten all the ripe fruit, the tender leaves, and even the bird eggs."

"And you haven't left any nuts for us," said Mangabey.

"I'm very sorry," said Chimpanzee. "I will save some food for you." And so Chimpanzee slowed his eating—for a day.

The monkeys called on Doondari. "You must take away Chimpanzee's tail so that he cannot climb so high," they begged. "He is starving us."

"I cannot take away what I have given," said Doondari. "You must stop Chimpanzee yourselves."

Vervet, Mangabey, and the other monkeys decided to call upon Crowned Eagle, the king of birds, who snatched monkeys from treetops. Their fear of Crowned Eagle was small compared with their loathing for gluttonous Chimpanzee.

"Tell me why I should not eat you now!" screeched Crowned Eagle when Vervet awoke him from a nap.

"You could, but then all the monkeys would disappear and you would die," said Vervet.

"Explain this," said Crowned Eagle.

"You see," said Vervet, "Chimpanzee is eating all the food, and soon the rest of us will starve. With no monkeys, you would go hungry as well."

"I see," said Crowned Eagle. Crowned Eagle flew to the highest treetops, where Chimpanzee was gorging himself on bird eggs and fruit. He was so busy eating that he did not see Crowned Eagle. Suddenly, Chimpanzee felt a searing pain in his rump and felt himself being lifted high above the canopy.

"Chimpanzee, you are a glutton," Crowned Eagle screeched. "I will not allow you to starve the monkeys. I think you will make a tasty meal for my hatchlings."

"Oh, no!" cried Chimpanzee. "This cannot be!" He twisted and wriggled madly, tearing himself loose of Crowned Eagle's claws. As Chimpanzee fell, he saw that his tail and the fur of his rump were still in Crowned Eagle's clutches. Chimpanzee landed with a crash, his rump in agony. To this day, Chimpanzee, who vowed to never climb very high again, has a red rump and no tail.

GLOSSARY

abstract – existing as a thought or idea without any physical representation

cognitive – relating to the mental process of gaining understanding through experience, thought, and the senses

deforestation – the clearing away of trees from a forest

dexterity – skill or agility in using the hands or body to perform tasks

displacing – being forced to leave one's home due to destruction or disaster

diverged – developed in a different direction

DNA – deoxyribonucleic acid; a substance found in every living thing that determines the species and individual characteristics of that thing

evolve – to gradually develop into a new form

extinct – having no living members

genetic – relating to genes, the basic physical units of heredity

gestation – the period of time it takes a baby to develop inside its mother's womb

impoverished – poor, or living in poverty

mammals – warm-blooded animals that have a backbone and hair or fur, give birth to live young, and produce milk to feed their young

metabolism – the processes that keep a body alive, including making use of food for energy

nomadic – relating to a group of people or animals with no fixed home who move, often according to the seasons, in search of food, water, or grazing land

orbit – to revolve around a body in space, such as a planet or star

poaching – hunting protected species of wild animals, even though doing so is against the law

zoologists – people who study animals and their lives

SELECTED BIBLIOGRAPHY

Campbell, Christina J., Agustin Fuentes, Kathrine C. MacKinnon, Simon K. Bearder, and Rebecca M. Stumpf. *Primates in Perspective.* 2nd ed. Oxford: Oxford University Press, 2010.

Goodall, Jane. *Through a Window: My Thirty Years with the Chimpanzees of Gombe.* Boston: Houghton Mifflin Harcourt, 2010.

Great Ape Trust. "Chimpanzees." http://www.greatapetrust.org/great-apes/chimpanzees/.

Jane Goodall Institute. "Chimpanzees." http://www.janegoodall.org/chimpanzees.

Lonsdorf, Elizabeth V., Stephen R. Ross, and Tetsuro Matsuzawa, eds. *The Mind of the Chimpanzee: Ecological and Experimental Perspectives.* Chicago: University of Chicago Press, 2010.

Westoll, Andrew. *The Chimps of Fauna Sanctuary: A True Story of Resilience and Recovery.* Boston: Houghton Mifflin Harcourt, 2011.

Chimps demonstrate sharp curiosity and enthusiasm for life— signs of a remarkable intelligence.

INDEX